Meme Measure

Meme Measure

Rich Murphy

RESOURCE *Publications* · Eugene, Oregon

MEME MEASURE

Copyright © 2022 Rich Murphy. All rights reserved. Except for brief quotations in critical publications or reviews, no part of this book may be reproduced in any manner without prior written permission from the publisher. Write: Permissions, Wipf and Stock Publishers, 199 W. 8th Ave., Suite 3, Eugene, OR 97401.

Resource Publications
An Imprint of Wipf and Stock Publishers
199 W. 8th Ave., Suite 3
Eugene, OR 97401

www.wipfandstock.com

PAPERBACK ISBN: 978-1-6667-9679-7
HARDCOVER ISBN: 978-1-6667-9678-0
EBOOK ISBN: 978-1-6667-9680-3

07/08/22

Otolith: "Confetti Catcher" and "Smile"

BlazeVox: "Progress"

Word For/Word: "Echo Answer," "Narcissus in Wilderness," and "Gospel"

Crosswinds Poetry Journal: "Foil Toil"

Grey Sparrow Literary Journal: "Red Letter Day"

Book of Matches: "The Trigger Range"

Terror House Magazine: "Cave man," "Flint Offerings"

Fixator: "Tornado Dodgers"

Dyst Literary Journal: "Adventures in Capitalism"

Last Stanza Poetry Journal: "Biochem Lab" and "Memegram"

Experiential-Experimental-Literature: "Night at the Opera," "Traffic Address," and "Course Obstacle."

In memory of my parents

> Mimetic attraction is bound to increase with the number of those who converge on one and the same antagonist. Sooner or later a snowball effect must occur that involves the entire group minus, of course, the one individual, or the few against whom all hostility focuses and who becomes the "scapegoats," ...
>
> —RENE GIRARD

Contents

Desire Contagion

Confetti Catcher | 3
Grace Note | 4
Smile | 5
The Trigger Range | 6
Horse Power | 7
Progress | 8
Freaking Fomentation | 9
Cloned Backbones | 10
Swank Rank | 11
Adventures in
    Capitalism | 12
The Unicyclist | 13
Viral Load | 14
Anti-Viral Punch Lines | 15
Inside Out Sex | 16
Course Obstacle | 17
Traffic Address | 18
Night at the Opera | 19
Likewise and So On | 20
Ruby and Ignatius TLA | 21

Marginalia

Cobbling Headquarters | 25
Snapshot: No. 1 in the Wild
    West | 26
Tongue Twister | 27
Dominoes in America | 28
Foil Toil | 29
Tornado Dodgers | 30
Planting Two Feet on
    Earth | 31
Altared States continued | 32
I Isles | 33
Sentence Structures | 34
Meme Kiosk | 35
Cartography for
    Beginners | 36
The Dogged Celebrity | 37
H.R. Department | 38
Corpus Orgini | 39
Metrics for Hysterics | 40

Dopamine Dunces

No Dominion | 43
Posturing Post | 45
Sin Skin in the Game | 47
Trash Talking | 48
Me Meme | 49
Rescue Scene | 50
Cycle Shop | 51
The Code Fold | 53

Hail Seizure | 54
Maybe Magnate | 55
Ta-Da Ta-Da Ta- | 56
Seer in the Main Frame | 57
! | 58
Starting Points | 59
Echo Answer | 60
Narcissus in Wilderness | 62
High-Seas Refrain | 63
Ear Worm | 64
Two-Step | 65
The Gear for a Way | 66
Cannonball, Swan | 67
Just Practice Makes Perfect | 69

Culture Climate Change

Swan Songs | 73
Playing with Matches | 75
Pantomime Sift | 76
A Metaphor Mimesis Ministry | 77
Civilizing Buzzwords | 78
Memegram | 80
Biochem Lab | 81
Cave Man | 82
Glass Half Empty | 83
Prescription for the Master | 85
Flint Offerings | 86
Mooning at the Glitter | 87
How to Become a Model | 88
O Day | 89
Meme Planet | 90
Becoming | 91
Red Letter Day | 92

Desire Contagion

"We desire what others desire because we imitate their desires."

"The distance between Don Quixote and the petty bourgeois victim of advertising is not so great as romanticism would have us believe."
—RENÉ GIRARD

"[P]oetry is a part of philosophy itself."
—ALAIN BADIOU

Confetti Catcher

Always the same site
with similar pomp and circumstances.
An organ shifts beneath flutes and violins
that blanket a dark band
tweaking noise into nose.

Cornea eggs crack in socket bowls
when stirring, and a gathering
quakes on the bed refrain.
When the sight ceremony lights up,
all dreams exit through thin air.

A whole world opens for the real
while boredom fills with illusion
for strangers on the street perhaps.

The senses chase after stomach butterflies
with a cup for coffee and a spoon.
The excitement wishes by as the moment
escapes, but the effort fills up
and spills all over the nervous system.

Soon a traffic jam will spread on
concentration without absorbing
a small part in the procession.

Grace Note

Strapped to backs,
the virtuoso grand pianos
haul through each day, each night.
Practice and playing frame
and tease in antiquity museums.
The next meal gathers
into focus raw talent while energy
hungers from desire to fingertips.

The key, if any tonic triad,
steals from other heaver ivories
the tinkling and pounding
while Main Streets, sidewalks,
and back-alleys rock and roll
in movements to a universe coda.

Pop and fizz from a champagne bottle.

The heavy dark cloud above,
lugged from birth to the other end,
knows by heart the private
coffin top crescendo and morendo.

Smile

When in pockets or on wrists
little wheels with teeth
gnashed through small lives,
the sidewalks lipped up
regardless, "have a nice day."

Then the coltan digit brought
to pitch in light speed.
Emoji and Gif poke into each cheek.
Tagging antisocial question marks
as coat racks for the street,
the command threatens to punish
insightful resisters at the cash register.

With time, a commuter buys into debt
or hunts for a refrigerator box
and a subway grate.

Even in confrontation with weather,
the baseline syndrome sufferers cling
to exteriors though from around brainstems
leather sacks for rotted emotions droop.

The Trigger Range

Victimized at Fort Coddle,
where books go unread
and experience sleeps late
into young adulthood,
the vapidity veteran installs
for anxiety, so word and image trigger.

Fear and desire shoot at tin cans
in train station waiting rooms
and on office building reception desks.

With every charge, a miss a ricochet
and the tenderfoot character
chases after retirement via middle age.

In Tome Town, the dream world
buys up mountains, rivers,
oceans, and cities.
Empathic impulses pump for the heart.

On the How-To Express, body limbs
and resilience seek out muscle and memory
for engagement for devotion.

Clicking, swiping, liking
insure the untouched shallow
when someone's death calls for hello help.

Horse Power

The pistons, invidious comparison
and mimetic desire, kick over
when a child first clutches a nickel
and don't lack fuel until well after death.

First-natures bare teeth
in envy and resentment,
and the economic engine
drives through centuries
and through the crowds on sidewalks.

Brooms also sweep up
accessorized personal effects.

Avoiding city streets
steers down country roads,
stares down impulse and addiction,
perhaps, but a seatbelt buckles up
the selfish effigy for conscience merely.
Good old greed floors the gas pedal.

The Joneses remain in a foxhole
across the cow path in parade uniforms:
The branding exercise for competition.
A gadfly in the exurbs exhausts
before the horse takes on a rider.

Progress

The costumer, shackled
in the needs-chain, shuffles
in lockstep along serial dairy products,
canned soup, and the extraction
time-line check-out points.

New and improved,
a believing owner digs
deeper into credit card debt
and pay day loans
while a siphon sucks up
into private jets and gated havens.

At every turn, desire trips
on good enough or over pie-in-the-sky.
After the fall, Mr. Please wakes
to a dozen begs quivering
for more upon the pouting lower lip.

From rice bowl to a house
in the burbs, want droops, a sack
over belts churning and growling
for a bite . . . for taste.

Freaking Fomentation

The overlords in the cockpit
ride the silicon jet stream
to the bull market
while the popup shops muster
and masked-anonymous
little peeps fend off disease.
Sky-written and punctuated
with gigs and branding exercises,
the future showers into satellite
dishes for the owned:
Nickels ping into a pan
and dimes evaporate into a cloud.
Neighborhood crooks mix
and match in desperation.
When trajectories time
for internal affairs,
engineers arrive to jimmy
a Jimmy into a pelvic space.
Control freaks with money
bet that despair disappears
with the petty people aping.
Plucking the genome from evolution,
the petting-zoo maintenance team
blueprints Homo cul-de-sac.

Cloned Backbones

Crisped and juiced with high IQs
and talents tweaked galore,
ersatz bipeds rise from the Gnome DNA
that once stood in reserve, gnomes.

Any original mutt on two legs left upright
clowns around trucking trash,
a spectator unto extinction.

Dolls, action figures, mannequins forecasted.

When raw materials
(minerals, four-legged species) deplete,
Jujitsu demands next in line for strip mining.
Up the double helix dashing Simulacra Sam
arrives on the scene to live the new healthy.

Cirrhosis and spleens idle
in dictionaries under "lame"
or pin to a waxed tray
for grade school biology class.

Shrinking global sapiens over-population,
the substitute creature elite,
the extra-terrain vehicle,
delivers to address affairs
between scarce goods and a hot sun.

Swank Rank

Neighborhood conspicuous
consumption Sumo wrestlers,
Flash Morgan and Sore-Eye Jones,
substitute for freedom vertigo.
Desire competitors mire in place,
status states where whole nations vote
to race tenement rats.

The petty jealousies and envy teams,
patrolling city limits
semaphoring in trendy knockoffs,
hunt for scapegoats to shame.

To care scares for showoffs
and the mimes in lower classes too.
The panic attack seethes and teethes,
whether through laughter
or the smile with quiet violence
that offers the street as a home.

Joining the swank rank and gloat
eats at days and decades
until a grave swallow.

Adventures in Capitalism

Ad ventures graffiti cities,
screen national news stream scenes,
and slap down any potential
meditative state, so that

desires herd into a death valley
where mountain tops pool desert.
Minds with heads prune into mirages
for even wolves showing off sheep skins.

Bleat (good, service) chains
into platitude and cliché.

While other outlets for creative breath
and hands remain within brain
subterranean reaches,
meme factories and markets squander,
and human generations and raw materials
disappear from the solar system, waste products.

Where practice meets in process,
the escape hatch opens
for a ready journeyman to master
as the empire lays claim to the backyard.

A thirsty carcass thinks back
to an early disability that needs
long-term compensation and over-compensates
again and again to achieve
freedom from baking in the sand.

The Unicyclist

After dogging behind in various classes,
a copy-cat berets convention
to swing aesthetic to hound
the unimaginative noggin.

Yes, yes, the beat loser
leaves for coffee break and never returns,
but the example just may embed.
The monkey-see-monkey-do gathering
on a planet thumps on bongos perhaps
should a cool thumb wish to drum.

The parakeets chime in so
that feathers don't fly back at a nest.
The next we know the old encyclopedia
gives way to a new bleating for memory
and song and accompanying bells.

A finger-popping flock
clichés around town wearing macramé
and watching for trends
in hope that a new bend in the road
guides the block-headed scat lover.

Viral Load

Passing through the state Self Love
when capitalism and the independence
illusion clouded rosy, a garden tomorrow,

a two-legged virus member
rubs at eyelids in disbelief
at the "individual" lie
only recently gone by.

Among the lesser fevers crawling
or sprouting, the reptilian brain-stem illness
branches into deadly limbs that preyed
on everything under the sun.

Fine-tuned under a black and blue sky,
the super-spreader predator still punishes
with extinction and gutted mountains.

The sea vomits, the wind whines
and wheezes while nations infect earth
with the contagion that burns into ash.

Extreme, whether summer or winter,
the industrial atmosphere commands,
and one-by-one the minions follow.

Anti-Viral Punch Lines

Laughter-rationing substitutes
for spontaneous guffaws, giggles,
toothy smiles that freed states
from perpetual boredom to disease hot zone.

Internal skeleton emojis scare from skulls
irony and sarcasm rescue efforts.

Microbe-load upon fossil-fuel addiction
wipes that grin from faces.
Virus added to virus plants feet
reaping isolation cells and straight-man death.

Locked down, dawn until dawn
and nowhere to drive steel and plastic
rolling on synthetic rubber,
the allotted lips and hips couched
in sweatpants address at home.

The prisoners mask wild imaginations
binge-watching television
where for wine-ladled coffee mugs,
space rocks, sit-com and drama
stretch latex titillation across oceans.

Shrunk to a beach stone, the planet
rests for a hard look that produces
little laughing matter.

Inside Out Sex

Gene memes march down the aisle
inside mimetic desire to advertise
and to warn: Match but seek elsewhere.

The romance in such a marriage
makes for more Homo sapiens.

Should the evolved ape fall in love
with any mother or father,
hell-rivals hail on Earth.

But the pre&post parental pattern
replicates resemblances
for most who attend to sacrifice
in communities and nations.

Safe in the cockpit, the future-pilots
wish to fill up living room
around the planet with replicas.

The flight to nowhere but here
brings up short the lone species, shoulder
to shoulder suffering suffocation.

Course Obstacle

Obstacles call for accessories
and designer zippers today:
Think Velcro for the elderly.
Challenges that would prod at
dreamland for tools and compensation
don't enter into Toyland heads.

Puffed men in stuffed chairs
altar the frivolous behavior
and the congregation kneels.
The nonbeliever scapegoat pool
pitch tents and needs and die
as designated off road vehicles
during the schlump movement
from recline to decline in America.

Morning stretches for soma-lax
professionals who finger keys
and move cursers around screens,
the game for the compound in exurbia.
Chased by the rising tides, non-player
characters (refugees and immigrants)
drown in razor wire, rifle butts, and sun.

News lights up celebrities for fools.

Traffic Address

In passing, the ongoing oversight
surveillance committee ignores
that long ago the two love tunnels
turned into parking lots without bottlenecks
or utility detail detours,
bringing passage to standstill.
The fog rolled in selling red and white canes.

Desire monitors wave on the coming traffic
and vehicles carrying cargo on other expressways.
Of course, snake oil barkers and more vicious
distraction manufacturers for world debt
circle around exterior dopamine corridors.

The nose and tongue spice up
the environs, and ears add ambiance:
horns and miniature violins.

The granite buckle, Appease Mountain,
that once dwelt for long moments
(maybe with caves) on tectonic plates
and in blue sky suffers from a confused state
brought on by leaders representing big business.

Night at the Opera

The invisibility simulator falls in love
with an emoji to marry social media
and disappears into ideology.

Bedding in white sheets every night,
dreams built for paradise and hell
until the sleeper mimed an angel
when the sun comes around.

Cellophane rolls crowd on sidewalks.
Whizzing cars with no one inside, beep!
World harmony, the same note,
sighs, and a tragedy plays on
as a romantic comedy.

A curtain drops with a thud
on every ending at the playhouse
before the ushers go to work
from the box office to emergency exits.

The audience members go
through the motions
as do stagehands and actors.

Likewise and So On

Every ditto in the cities yawns
at dawn in harmony over identities lost
or never obtained and owned.

The synchronized sleepwalking
citizens eggshell when smartphones
crack eyelids on curbstone edges.

The likewise and so on pool:
redundant simulacra abundance.

Ballet leg prompts
follow behind cadence action
and eggbeater kicking stimulants
(can-can sardines in cans),
highlighting conspicuous exclusion
for any sidewalk audience member.

With so many etceteras stomping,
toward some point, the copycats
and mime parades weigh down
the planet that could slips
from orbit around the sun.

Ruby and Ignatius TLA

Desire drools from a distance
and disappears when furnished
finally with living room:
Two yardsticks nailed together
and stuck into an arm pit
bend under the wait.

Dreamers slip and slide
on saliva a lifetime
without learning from any fall.
Sneakers fill with feet, muscle,
and a breath held for miles.

(The dopamine dealer and the dupe
exchange unseen on the street corner.)

Once the imagination finishes
painting an utopian landscape
and people enter the scene,
an old ladder round pokes in fun.

A rug pulls out from under progress:
Ruby Amnesia who embarrasses
a personality growth spurt.
Even Ignatius Quigley (IQ) runs down
wishes to wash dirty dishes daily.

Marginalia

"In Western nations, and above all in the United States, it animates not only economic and financial life, but scientific research and intellectual life as well . . . .

"The true threat to the world today comes from the mad ambitions of states and capitalists bent on destroying non-modern cultures. It is the so-called developed countries that plunder the planet's resources without showing the least concern for consequences they are incapable of foreseeing."
—RENE GIRARD

"[T]hose who do not make themselves continuously available for synchronous stress seem asocial."
—PETER SLOTERDIJK

Cobbling Headquarters

At the social construction site,
necks crane, zeitgeist projections
onto cave-wall manuals step
toward a choreography for people,
and earth movers sometimes
seem to move Earth.
Fear and desire traipse or dance
around outside the hospital wings
where inside patient thinkers
pace up and down corridors
or sit in rooms alone
drawing concepts from a wellness.
Without foundation, without concrete
plans, without cement mixers,
hard heads spread rumors and mimes
to form a convention center
that sticks to conduct or larynxes.
When the basic notions cure
into fallback catchalls
and background settings,
freedom opens up landscape
with paths and guardrails
for the philosopher itching
to leave the sanatorium.
Hardhats, now prisoners,
in guard uniforms man towers
after obeying traffic signals
and punching into work on time.

Snapshot: No. 1 in the Wild West

The self-absorbed bloat steals from compassion:
A sponge owning an ocean, crannies, sacks,
and surfaces savoring the seven seas.
When energy, sharing in a community, lounges,
an ego fattens enough to boast and taunt.
One mirror distorts against neighbors
and can focus on a blemish, a navel for days
without well water threatening the smile.

A continent suffering from a "wide open spaces"
delusion: fields for flag and amber waves,
distance runners, and elbows, stretch across maps.
100 million dynamo blame-siphons tap into 250
million meager moped engines who need
embracing that doesn't sap fuel tanks.
In a land where amour de soi overruns
in gated homes, in private schools,
in finance and business, spectacle promotion
warns in carefully maintained slums.

Tongue Twister

A host sits on a knee to learn a second language.
Throwing nouns and verbs to distract sense,
the ventriloquist steals from a people
who suspect valuables are disappearing.

Sentences and head movement mimicry
from the dummy mean little to the thief
(pantomimes don't do),
though much later redemption will be sought.

Until then, a parasite kicks around second class sapiens.

Keeping up appearances in both,
the blockheads with two social systems
attempt to master one while dropping the other.

The jugglers entertain for the sleepy cheerleaders
who lack talent and rest on privilege and goods.

While a few trainees reap for memory and a present,
an impossible multi-task practice
and may even buffoon the magic show comedian,
self-inflicted genocide hangs in the air
(liquor, diabetes, despair) for any bi-lingual survivors.

Dominoes in America

Alligator meat that survived 800 teeth
came out to the street to confront
white supremacist police.

During open season site training
(wink wink nod nod) long-skilled
targets run until viral shots
bring hoodies in the hood to knees,

and revenge against the security guard
who in aisle nine measures the distance
between poverty and desperation
from should to shoulder.

Tear ducts spray open;
rubber rounds whistle and pepper
from barrels; and batons twirl
to break bones until reptiles
and inflatable tokens litter
within the scapegoat pool.

Foil Toil

Wielding gaslight,
the professional wealth extractors
divide within poor neighborhoods
after laying pipelines.

Some drip-plumbing spills, clangs
when black and white clash
in stealth or in the streets.

Learned helplessness
and self-loathing teams
police through the race line.

While maintaining the scapegoat pool,
employed custodians in shabby custom
praise through official owner-song
and accompanying violence:
"You will not replace us" alarms.

Not punching up but kicking down
wins for the day (or evening) every time.

Even as institutions collapse brick
and mortar around the national façade,
the penitentiary yard that replaced
the cotton fields weathers.

Tornado Dodgers

The trailer park resident
waits at a forever detour for a thank you
from a gated compound privilege.
Suburban and urban dwellers
contribute to the joke butt
by retreading in public canned sitcoms.

Flooring an accelerator
on the extraction principals,
a high roller cartoon character
takes, only, too busy to hail a cab
or to let up on the poor.

Government regulatory administrators
tire while sitting in the emergency vehicle
with four flat tires and a bumper dimple.
The red tape that comes with a legislative bill
doesn't hold long before private sector
moths eat loopholes for trucks.

And pathways to wealth for clerks exhaust:
Promotion to a hedge fund right hand
wears down shoe leather too
but worth the deadening exercise.

"Trash" piles just off the highway
for the eventual blind sacrifice.

Planting Two Feet on Earth

For the crowd
standing-in to judge for authenticity,
fitting-in mocks regardless
though the privileged substitutes
often skip rehearsals.

All the while, the mimesis contestants
abandon interior origins
for what the Simon Sez mechanics
in the daily class exercises.

Caught in a double-bind,
the awkward imitators then face
that the charade uproots,
and drama coaches for psyches
for both depth and surface rivals
call for rotten tomatoes;
fans and cheer-leading squads quit.

Common ground remains
under feet for Homo sapiens,
blind without comparison.

Altared States continued

In the gas-lit nation,
citizens trip over facts day or night,
bruising measurements
and crippling judgment.
Sometimes a laceration
from the previous year bleeds
onto new friends
or a broken vision
from the past meat-grinds
the future horizons into a bowl
for sausage-making intestines.
The truth lamps wink
and twinkle at the naïve
and for the too-busy-to-think.
Whole groups flash-mob
with baseball bats to beat
pulp from neighbors:
Nursing homes spoon-feed mush.
Hypno-reality run-amok
illuminates through senses
while amputees feel around
for phantom trunks,
while facial recognition fun
ignites for algorithms
and police round ups.
Violence flails to ID a scapegoat.

I Isles

Signaling a virtue from island
to island, an archipelago armada
defends against other fidelity claims
that sail among to harbor.

Each fleet, faithful to a message
sent by semaphore or dog whistle,
mops up decks with cannon fodder:
Gas lighting and name calling.

Litmus tests assess before the gullible
board the convention hulls for initiation
and tattoos that anchor into position.
Who goes there: flesh or foul?

To hell with vision for a planet!
Surface identity party hats,
surgical masks, and noise makers
take over seven sea troubled waters.

Muck wrestling teams rake
for a chance at the keynote speech
as the relay baton passes forward
a continent away from a drunk.

Sentence Structures

Local communities cross over current events
upon the rotting foot-bridge slats
platitude, cliché, and memes.
Aided by tone, body language, and virtue signals,
the dunked may survive drinking too much,
bobbing among the rocks, dropping from a fall.

A few ginger dance-steps light-foot
for the other side to understand enough.
An old joke trestles where irony buckles.
Sometimes a rhythm carries for an earth-mover
providing meaning or more, experience.
Who knows how the dirt-filled bucket
maneuvers from one side to the other?
A disbelief-suspension overpass miracle.

World affairs sweep under worn troupe treads
for the fortunate naïve speech figure
and drown out gurgles and cries for help.
Boiler plate buzz and vapid verbs
perform for minding business as usual:
The morning lover escapes
from the everyday emergence angst.

Meme Kiosk

Trend-setters in neighborhoods
barely outpace the envy and resentment
that threaten to overtake the freedom
to keep up with the Joneses.

From pillow-top to Dollar Store bobble
progress thrashes beyond horizons
for fast money from addicted
credit card holders in every community.

The hungry and roofless debt-slaves
tap into nature where redundant K-9s
and shivering pelts prey upon family,
friends, and apparent wealthier strangers.

The Voltaire Church collapsed
onto the faithful around strip malls,
online shopping sites, and Wall Cheat.
Streets fill with disillusioned flock.

Cartography for Beginners

Where memes collide,
nations stretch out the razor wire
and station border guards.
One might may mumble;
another might may stomp.
Five senses divine
for ends and beginnings.

Interrupted inhabited habits –

when the symbols clash,
the bands on both sides battle
from house to hovel
(from march to hobble)
in neighborhoods
to exercise individual rites –
sometimes the last.

The flags planted in ruts
headed to cemeteries
grow in celebration each year.
The blossoms burst in the night sky:
A pedestal rocking God to sleep.

A dark day falls on every garden once,
a sacrifice to repetition.
Worshipers face up to heavy eyelids.

The Dogged Celebrity

Beyond a hassock, the best friend
barks and gestures at two human senses.
The leash clips onto couched eyes
that gawk, a tail wagging
for adventure at a tale wagging.

Burying bones in shallow plots
and in cushy screenplay lines,
the loyal mutt in sweats channels.
A remote-controlled day news soap
binges into the nighttime news saga.

With no need to compare a yawn
to a forager on a garbage heap
or refugee wearing Nikes,
a basset hound in the suburbs
wrinkles into a dreamland escape.

The vicarious animal dresses
in costumes only and pants
until a laundry pile substitutes
for a full life acted upon:
"Woe, for the world."

H.R. Department

The genius also fakes to make.
Step one: Talent and wound inventory;
step two: Pick one and practice.

Fools and tools name to shield
against practice and polish,
while standing in reserve
at the assembly line fortune
for someone else.
The pressure from concerns
outside head and heart interiors
shambles to assure
no self-design for a lifetime.

Undistracted by fast-cash need,
the inside-out children promote
through adulthood without saying a word.

Slow to catch-on the gig worker
plays American baseball,
sliding into every employment base
before any dream convinces
living without garage stuffers
wins over owning home plates.

Slower still technology as a lens
opens up possibility for essential states
not with extension for extension
but with craftsmanship.

Corpus Orgini

Usually, an emergency determines
when an organist goes to church:
on a gurney to a surgeon behind an altar.
An annual physical examination
calls for a blessing by a scale,
stethoscope, and a prick to a finger.

Meeting flesh along the way
bones point out a way forward,
push on elevator buttons,
and poke at a keyboard.

Without a bow or accolade
the nine-to-five pipes-and-tissue
performer engages for sinners
a Sunday best on weekdays.

Exhaling with relief after the wear
and tears, rest and rest
(two long notes) pass on
without honor, respect, or notice
so that checklist / checkout wind boxes
align end with beginning.

Metrics for Hysterics

Should the honest emotion
confront an orange or egg
hairs stand on end,
nerves rattle kitchen knives,
hierarchical authoritarian options
present for a frontal lobe.
Instinct wakes on a planet.

Strait-jacketed in habit,
civil screen, and social custom
spinal-tapped, terror succumbs
to the shock absorbers.

A mother disowns and denies;

a neighbor butchers for dinner
and in pre-emptive self-defense

unless each morning
a meme crustacean forms
a coat of arms and legs,
a jumpsuit for the well-grounded.

The nudist streaks through town.

Dopamine Dunces

"[H]umans imitate one another more than animals, they have had to find a means of dealing with contagious similarity, which could lead to the pure and simple disappearance of their society. The mechanism that reintroduces difference into a situation in which everyone has come to resemble everyone else is sacrifice."

—RENE GIRARD

No Dominion

All authority lost,
death packs up ghosts,
skeletons, and scythe
and slinks beneath flower beds
crying "boo who."

For the commuter crowd,
the threatening finger wag
from nuclear warheads
and smart-bomb poundings
on lecterns in far off desert
and jungle villages
numb from the waist up.

With Hubble home movies
planted in one eye
and a high school microscope
lodged in the other
each Homo sapiens squirms
on a glass GPS slide.

The work-ethic applicant
pledges with debt
the coming and going
in cities to inoculate
insignificance that puts on shoes
and a show each morning.

After children hiding in closets
discover that mom and pop
have swung from tree to tree
for millennia, a kind virus
with limbs, adolescents
compete to live forever.

Posturing Post

When reading the spinal column each morning,
the hip ball-and-socket skips over
the headlines and stands up
wearing a beret and snapping fingers.
Each lumbar lug nut first vows to balance
bold font that wobbles on shoulders
before spinning saucers on a stick
at a nowhere-to-go job.

Caffeine kicks in with the two-step.

Soon swinging from a strap
with the funny page tickling under a shirt,
tender-hearted Will travels from brainstem
to coccyx and back on the Marrow Line
in the Nerves-End subway system.

Even if late in the afternoon
an organ-grinding masseuse
kneads along the boney Braille
to compose a chord for a cord (aahh),
the invertebral discs only click into place.
When the magic hands align or perhaps push,
tough guys and gals give and take
in the blind faith church for healthy living.

Laying down the persistence,
resilience, snaking from ass to skull,
basks in the dark on a mattress
dreaming stories ranging from rubber to steel.
Worshiping skin that survives
the desert journey under the sun,
the reptilian tent pole packs easily.

Sin Skin in the Game

Traveling somewhere along the optic nerve
and heading for the retina, light converts
from religious mystery to scientific fact,
via electricity for an isolated fragile dynamo.

By the time cerebral layers and occipital lobe
finish with the zaps and shocks trees and people
distinguish for the prefrontal cortex and language:
"God? Outsmarted," the complete thought goes!

The chips on shoulders wondered for 30 days,
every one a Sunday in need for an inhuman within,
and opened to hacking by corporate states:
New Yoke linking Boss-town to headquarters
in Washing-ton by the Silicon Highway.

Apps captured with a dopamine dash
for the algorithm that has daft mobs dancing
down Main Street where the mother board
wires to the brain stem and amygdala,
the names and addresses noted in milliseconds.

Trash Talking

The food for thought brings
on diabetes in the spirit.
Sweet dreams, junk living,
and cheap talk over time nurses
with a prick to test for a blood stream
inside the ignorant cynicism.
Quick meals served on platitudes
seduce with fill up promises,
drive through easy-tear cliché packets,
and paper napkins for excess
language oozing out mouth corners.

No good happens in reality.

The air waves and pixel points
wash down while a continent
steps on the gas from job to job.
Flabby assessments grease grousing.
Threats forest the middle finger
expressway that treats feasting eyes.
Cheez Whiz: condemned
to a long sentence with a colon!
An ideology that once leaned
on free enterprise and what hunger
tethers to a dialysis machine.
Language will not live long.

Me Meme

To inoculate against fingers pointing,
by noontime the narcissus factors in
a guilt gauge reading
beside a victims status needle
and balances on a faux eye-beam.

The gymnast in the tall not-me weeds
sends out camouflage, decoys,
friends, a stalling tactic until the winner,
not a sacrifice, emerges.

Bandaged for the victory laps alone
(and mirrorless) the predator in disguise
continues colonizing until a few
ducks align behind.

Not jaw-dropping awe from the masses
but planting thoughts enough
in the district gardens,
Dr. Self-Love props up the hierarchy.

Rescue Scene

Tangled in the worldwide animal web,
marionette fingers twitch
while worshiping heroes.

The blank dare-the-devil application forms
(urban legend, national savior, superstar),
practice opportunities for peace on Earth,
fill out a burgeoning gig economy
spurring on mad-dash debtors.

Three chairs—one for the dog trainer,
one for the cat sitter,
and one for the bus rider between jobs.
Small roles detail either side in a show,
Name the Bad Guy.

Buried in alibis and evidence minutia,
detectives suffocate in cultural innocence
as exhibit A, B, and C squirm in dirt.

All the while sacrificing nothing
the immortal gods buy, buy,
and the string section, suspended
in nature, plucks at bye-bye.

Cycle Shop

Side-by-side dopamine cycles
store in the hypothalamus.
Every fancy, dream, ideal
lines up in various colors,
sizes, and styles to tempt
and tease the horse power.
Carrots dance in heads first
before dollar-sign sketch-artist
pushers rat around incentive
factories and display windows.

Each vehicle, motorized
and cushioned under the fanny,
distracts for the desire anglers.
Neurons squirt onto sale sprockets
and marketer-imagined event chains.
Danglers study to master hypnosis
and eyeball response speeds,
fly-fishing for dollars.

Host Wanted, Alive if possible.
Rewards: Anticipation . . . ,
stimuli, and pleasure. Repeat.

The dire need to put suckers-
born-every-minute onto a tricycle
drives at Attention-Grabber Institutes.
An in-debt acrobat hovering

in balance over an 18-wheeler,
the brass ring for scientific brands,
cowboys products "Yeehaa" into dust.

Along the path to the Bigger-Than-One-
Self Horizon every once in a while
a unicycle embarks.

The Code Fold

Riding algorithms into the future,
the recursive parasite that builds hosts
never needs to practice again.
Robotics rumba and tango
and even nudge aside bosses.

Habit, assembly-line workers
go out the window forever.

A Wild West show discovers
when greeting contingency: "What's next"
face-to-face without masks, handles,
or netting for the buck or bronco. Gulp!

Straddling unemployed boredom
through a "work day," apathy opens
to nothing but surprise
butting consciousness without rut or end:
Attention grabs at any noon pajamas.

Eyes don't close for the layabout;
mirrors and the sun stare.
Purpose comes with explosives
to mine the mind, while desire
hammers at everything in sight.

Hail Seizure

After adopting the laws and rites
fingers and toes adapt
to the depression empire
where all skull vessels bow down
around the capitol, Amygdala.

The lightning brigade strikes
from headquarters to the exterior
and burns up any energy meant to thrust
independence to vassals.

Colonists from the furthest reaches,
redundant meme stand-ins without purpose,
collapse to knees and palms.

An oppressive armed sentry shoulders
every step along the sunny lanes.
Free from charge, each silver lining
comes surrounded by a gray, suicide crowd.

Mined by an out-going behavior specialist
that now pleads for reason,
the mind weighs on scales owned
by coulda-shoulda thumbs.
Each morning guilt reigns with a heave.

Maybe Magnate

With dopamine sitting at the right hand
wearing a daffy grin, Maybe rules
for planet Homo sapiens and the soma system.

The inhabitants (limbs, trunk, cranium)
worship at the local parish concerns
and arrive at chance happenings.
In time, rituals, prayers, and routine fasting
can draw out certainty one way or another.

Sometimes silence and stillness luck out
and god carries on shoulders for half a mile.
The Ferris-wheel peak plummets quickly.

Under the wacky smile, the desire
for anticipation calls in tongues from toe tips.
Whole worlds rush around to discern
which superstition works best –

given the footprints and the foot positions
on the ground . . . until copycats study
behind an OCD patient mime.

Each congregant seduces with a unique twist,
and Perhaps peeps through a thunderhead
throwing lightning this way and that.

Ta-Da Ta-Da Ta-

Before habit drones on and on
in a tucked nursing home bed
short-term wants huff and puff
at muscular / skeletal mobile structures,
balloons, each with a small hole:
"Why am I here?"

A lifetime desire fills up lungs
to fuel the heart so that practice
builds the muscle for the long
stay ahead at the cemetery.

Dance class or any daily exercise
involving feet, rhythm,
and a few chosen words
sets up the stages without props
for a more accurate ID.

Each challenge for tapper or swan
always pokes and prods for real,
for the authentic and genuine.
That good news allows
for a circus ring too far . . . .

The acrobat prays in thin air without a net.

Seer in the Main Frame

The fortune teller predicts
to the individual moment outcomes
for every life, mundane.
Relying on palm and mind readings,
the corporate state stares
with glazed eyes into azure to reign.
An unpredictable moment
with city routines breaking
lodges in a dream world.
Even the off-the-grid bumpkin
goes to bed at night.
Owning the tarot deck
and algorithmic gypsy costumes
simulation teams square off
around computer terminals.
Bankers pay for lip-service
from politicians but not a scent
leaks to losers Joe and Jamal.
The forecast blackens
when the genome draws
from the deck, and Ace of Pentacles
slips into the timetable.

!

A child surprises when hoppy
coincidence jumps on a pogo-stick!
A man subtracts from old
to unearth proto pronto.
Long dark days . . .
after a tragic accident simply
drag out ellipsis until lightning
strikes at some point again . . .
The electricity generated
by a zip-a-dee-doodah moment
sparks with promise only though.
But an embrace between
a wonderful ray and playground
giggles, picks up the guttered
and gutted for a minute, a day.
Without a spring, reasonable
grown-ups bet on an ellipse
that launches luck and blessing
while the ups and downs
for the skipping schoolyard
optimists bounce with magic.

Starting Points

Parrying to foil lunges
from rays or rain all day,
mines with picks for internal wells
and maps-out interior deserts.

Forehead wiping, eye rubs
five-times-a-minute to comfort
alone against environmental needling,
two porcupines approach
searching for a hand with relief.

Reading expressions face-to-face,
a flinch or blink, brings to ball bristle,
so en garde lines greet and court perhaps
for two brushes against the world
that uncurl a whole solar knot.

Two archer armies quivered mirror
in hope for only interlocking puzzle pieces,
while futures hinge on slings, arrows,
and improvised devotion vices.

Echo Answer

When magic drains from ritual,
the past disappears, so for loyalists
time repeats in habit.
Props and utensils lay about,
never touched again.

Performing CPR on a moment
long in the calendar trash pile,
the secret nostalgia coaxer
dances with blowup youth
in an inflated earlier environment.
Memory energizes for the senses
to bring the furniture to life.

The gone in the now
limps into tomorrow,
available for litany in a day,
parody in a week.

The novel threatens
until the sentimental liver
encroaches on OCD territory
that triggers the repeater
holstered in the brainstem.

A funeral procession concession
loosens up behavior dug
into favorite words and deeds
to provide a coffin lid
where stars once took on wishes.

The sun and moon
sweep away the check marks
and the possibilities
littered by a Homo sapiens.

Narcissus in Wilderness

In the ego mirror where the human
appears colossus from every angle,
the background reflects with honesty:
No conscience for what props
when the exaggeration trooper
living in a glasshouse stomps the wild.

The blown up twin dances
in a greenhouse where rocks
enter via a door and not a window.
Manners carry for the monstrous,
unsoiled, and innocent hands.
Meanwhile developers crowd out
for living room furniture
and bedroom sets, as the rooted uproots
and routed paws squeeze and blur
against photo frames.

Self-regarded into a god but lost
among mountains, oceans, and stars
the misrepresented hedonist
in circus tent shirt and two sacks for pants
discovers among the dying.

High-Seas Refrain

In the earworm belly
the intimidation and consolation
armed to the teeth
wait for the Trojans to close the gate
before seizing the political muscle.

A victory song that boosts
the youthful pride with rhythm
and spirited melody celebrates.

The pop music hook catches on
auditory membranes and nerves,
and while bringing home Helen,
a whole docile but capable generation
reels in dance and reels in.

A few years later a tv commercial
adopts the golden oldie gang
for deep fry fish and chips:
So many vessels never arrive
at Athens: Poseidon smiles.

On grocery aisles sirens wave;
the geeks always cheat.

Ear Worm

Airborne, the refrain germ
squirms into ears to hatch the worm
that measures into cliché the day.
Over and over a rut record hums
from a needled speaker with lips.

The cranium sound studio leaks
about from time to time,
so the less empathetic (perhaps
with similar cork-lined noggins)
hear through a voice box in bits and bars
that bare a no-show verse universe.

No tympanic membrane immerses
without risking a couch surfer to writhe
an audience member from head to toe.

Two-Step

While the environment taps a foot
to kill minute moments, genes meme:
Ticks swarm to line up and tic by.
Who knows where the background
music comes from, but the strings
catch on pants and the percussion
pounds within hearts from around stars.
Undeniable threads stretch into sunlight.

Though friendlier than desert orbs,
the crowded planet clambers with desire.
A dry patch bakes into an oasis
for dune lovers, in the meantime,
who slip on loafers at the multiplication table.
Variations on themes scamper under brush
or rise within trunks and limbs,
or climb upon hill and hump.

Helix staircases head to visibility and voice
from the basement apart ment where parties
itch to raise hell but find that carbon copies
Jane or Johnny will have to do.

The Gear for a Way

A long entourage trails off for city blocks
behind the coat tails manufacturer,
Welcome Aboard, now up in lights.
The hangers-on know that the train
doesn't stop and so hold on to hand straps
and super cape beliefs.

With the meritocracy mentoring
a thousand groupies
each class for a century incorporates
and furnishes for so-so followers
who wrap in appropriated glory.
Few run-a-ways would dare against confidence
in a direction away from crowds
to risk a path with material essentials alone.

A waist coat or vest sewing cycle
stitches in a small town in Buttonhole Valley.
For the tailored jacket wearer,
solitude sweetens for the focused mastering.

Cannonball, Swan

Snorkeling every day, all week
in a pool for the public,
a poet breathes in and out alone.
The tube breaking water
inserts into a mouth.

After a long day
at the social construction site,
lemmings in spandex
not already splashing
in the smartphone, edge
away from a dry crying towel
or line up at the diving board.

Any words not cliché,
or platitude sink, disappear
into thin blue liquid sand,
glass, before a swipe.
Once in the manmade lagoon,
few survivors escape
from the dopamine or ad apps
that add to a bottom line.

Every spritzer bubble bursts
to tell above a head: The tale,
either short or tall, but sweet.
Hurrying away from the drowning,
a lifeguard for tomorrow

realizes that vocabularies
interfere with each other
and invents to replace both.

The bard returns to the forever dunk
with wind pipe extensions and masks
for anyone seeking rescue.

Just Practice Makes Perfect

When a vexed biped fuses repeated
over-compensation to a personal debt
payment owed to Homo sapiens,

a sun bursts through to conduct with charge
the solar system and mix music with the galaxy.

A good habit wins for the race. YAY!

Eyes in the night light up
for an orchestrated lifetime effort.
Any gods in the area examine
again everything in nature.

The acrobat and artist,
placed on an Olympian pedestal
for children to mock and mimic, wink.

Only on the austerity altar,
where archeology will reveal
generations deformed for empire,
the roadmap to gene pool engineers
bathes in a glow for the moneyed self-selected.

Culture Climate Change

"Everyone can and even must be different, because ultimately differences no longer make any real difference. The extreme, the other and the wholly other are from now on only aesthetic categories . . ."

"What is required today is a readiness to play your role as a conductor of excitation for collective, opportunistic psychoses."
—PETER SLOTERDIJK

"Man is the creature who does not know what to desire, and he turns to others in order to make up his mind."
—RENE GIRARD

Swan Songs

Usually, the black swan
arrives with an archeologist,
a team spirit.
Approaching disasters
feather in more clearly
from a greater distance
thanks to a trowel, finds tray,
and fine point needle picks.

No song, no warning,
citizens adapt to slow changes
until frogs boil or coastlines
shore inland 100 miles or so.
Too late to choke off
the mammoth wingspan
and the dark days ahead,
the business minders
or experts in fields
swamp up to necks.

Even, if possible,
swimming for a homeland
without floatation devices
the surprised parties hug
on the way down
or flail until fail.

Poets with lines in graying water,
the fluffy silver spume,
gargle or garble for any heads up
to the few readers who
don't migrate in V formation.
The catch for the day
serves for larynx and eyes here.

Playing with Matches

A neighbor lets fly with a match
(twin lawns or look-a-like fences),
the green fire ignites,
and a city burns with envy
until every home escapes
into blazing stereotype.

The accelerant, cradled, capped,
and stored in the tribal lobe,
leaks into spray when pressed
by conformity and competition.

To avoid the goat on the altar
and a last bleating breath,
"me too" camaraderie spills.

The suspicious eyes poke and prod
at cliché to find originality traces
or unique character traits.
If not a ladder round higher
or abutting the income evidence,
catch up challenges
upon every drive home.

Small desires accessorize
to defend against listening to air
from lungs that wish to speak
the truth for the body and brain.

Pantomime Sift

The metaphor seismograph spikes
and eyeballs roll around
bumping against images
until a symbol amasses a focus
into place for a whole pop population.

New truth nails to repair a species.

Breath-taken, a continent crowd
then thrashes around for a little wind
in diaphragms to jumpstart and ignore
the unconscious monotony
within the ribcages from host to host.

The shifting plates, from cupboard
to ocean floor, settle into new
pie charts and tables unrecognized
at first heave and glance.

A parasite hides.

Fixing senses into a short-term
common sense each time the dog barks,
fleas dig in; the master heels.

A Metaphor Mimesis Ministry

> "What then is truth? A mobile army of metaphors, metonyms, and anthropomorphism"
> —FRIEDRICH NIETZSCHE

Toying for tools among the hills,
imaginations swarm to stretch
and discover within the science idea.

On the ball, hands too small to grip
and old-timer paws play at extending
the uses for found interstellar rock,
galactic water, and solar system air.

Eyeballs dive through microscope
tubes to swim with amoebas
or dance with subatomic particles.

No one yet knows how far sapiens
can go in both directions.
But the ice caps have been cocked
wise guy style and a pandemic
corners heroes with a snub-nosed 38.

The doctors in the lab throw around
beanbags but not at face value really . . .
so long as money pours into blood banks
and hedge funds IV poles balance
and the privileged on Earth win.

Civilizing Buzzwords

When metaphor memes after standing
on feet and dancing or rattling the cage
in prose, the light still throws into the wild.

Pointing stops though, and the handles
that come with symbols catch
onto palms going to market.

The touchstone flourishes,
for instance among the bushel baskets
and the animals hanging on hooks
to attract cash through eyes:
Flowers, flowers everywhere . . . .

While everywhere the truth solidifies
within every sense, the way
to tomorrow clears for whole nations.

Thinkers poke for improvement
or applaud at rhymes and mimes.

Regardless, in time
cliché bores in on dwellers

who then punch holes in simile
and allegory, the dark lies that fill
the starless space just beyond the nose.

With no image to own or parody,
soon ideal identities audition
for trope runoffs and crowds
listen for an echo or a catchy ring.

Memegram

A variation on a meme,
sent out from the planet, shakes
at the international sand art.

The Earth quake erases
to begin again with truth,
perhaps one that bridges enough
to lived experience for a century or so.

Grounded over-sized brains
assert, explore, disavow on two feet.

The gravity throughout the process holds
onto great expectations for a species
scratching granite while lost in space.

Though the upside down etch-a-sketch
mirrors beach and desert
and attracts gray areas under a sun,
transparent plastic breaks down after a cry.

Biochem Lab

After the volcanoes choked on virgins
to appease the gods and first born
did the trick keeping the death numbers
down for awhile for cultures, old goats
stuck out necks for whole communities.

Then finally, the world shrank
for the people who brought the bucket.
And as though the sailors and families
believed that the color-sacrifice
sufficed as innocent enough

entire races morphed into rotten eggs
and were thrown under buses
a dozen-at-a-time all day, every day.

From bone broth and muscle greed
the primordial soup fed carrot and sticks
and seasoned with resentment, winter, envy.
The jellyfish able to take shapes
set foot on shore and never looked back
for empathy, cooperation, imagination.

Cave Man

Within the echo chamber,
where shadows support the byte,
reports from the battle for dollars
keep on the lights with rhythmic
shocks through electronic hearths.

The ol' time religion dies
with much whimpering
at the chorus by the congregation.

Outside the concerted hall
the sock puppets continue to rule
with science spearheading
inquests and expeditions.
Shoulder upon shoulder,
elephant upon turtle, tools rumble
from earth mover to tweezers
that don't quite meet to pinch.

Without the cosmos in a capsule
the brain bunks alone only
to greet a mirror when dawn breaks:
Without gray matter in stark relief
and verifiable during becoming
stars spin out from the senses.

Glass Half Empty

The bottle washer
and noble interior minister
rides on reptile shoulders,
insisting the reins function.

Fresh swamp miasma wafts
from clothing though intent letters
provided for safe passage
from Neanderthal landscapes.

The jerking left and right
along the graded slalom road test
failed to leave on the highway
one detour cone standing—Hooot!
Scales and horn weigh in:
A loaded 18-wheeler
without brakes, without steering.

The innards within seven billion
species members wait,
while scrubbing tonic containers,
for evolution to turn over a tarot card.

Conscience and consciousness
dress up in a diplomat uniform
that clinks empty on door stoops
or rattles in recycling bins.

Homo sapiens genes spill when practicing
statesmanship on the way to transparency:
Envy, resentment, schadenfreude ferment.

Prescription for the Master

From first tear to last sigh,
the cliché puts up with
pot and pan administrations.

Deep state to deep cleaners,
lines form at the rear.
When at the grocers,
no rare bird or beast with identity
carts around plastic-wrapped aisles.

The spoons drumming
upon the blackened metal bottoms
call to table where paradise
feeds smiles all around,
the latest shadows on a wall
for the chain-smoked.

Dumming-down to wake up
the casters in the media
to a not knowing honesty
puts in danger artists
whether plugged in or not.

Needled and then pinned
to a canvas, the philosopher points
to a way out, but terrified
at the prospect, state janitorial staff
keeps the house lights on.

Flint Offerings

Charred stick piles substitute
for grave stones in cemeteries:
Death matches after consumption.

Electronic screens strike at desire
to ignite momentary delight
that soon burdens attics, garages, sidewalks.

Whole families tunnel deeper
and deeper into debt: The Family Plot,
the daisy plan dug under consciousness.

Generation after generation,
while false needs torched hearts
and nerve endings with death-denying tricks,
misses out on the talent shows.

For the protagonist at "The End"
the ta-da illusion stuns, takes breath away.

The solitary "Hurray" awakens
for every sun master who springs
from inability to over-compensation.

Mooning at the Glitter

The poet rattles at cell doors,
sucks on a binky, and cries
when nursery rhymes end.
The Bastille cellar brat
prays for each foot
to twinkle in the night sky
when the menu offers
only dirt for every meal.

From motherhood get-go
mutation limitation eats
at future balladeering flesh.
Each song leads to a gong,
and the reader still in
merely a little older skin.
Desire for development
invents until a denial basket
floats down the Nile
or brainwashes upon
the Mississippi banks.

With fingers plugging at
the keys in seeming Everland
the hermitage construction
built from spores and bacteria
grows up a cellular type A-Z
personality that punctuates
an organism wishing
on the spaces between the stars.

How to Become a Model

Pattern creators evolved
from collectors who rummaged
through chaos for matches
between current affairs
and personal family impressions.

The fleshy outer drum
and psyche butterfly wings span
to take in the planetary atmosphere.
All interruptions record for a lifetime.

Exploration and discovery
take on a lifetime for display
cases often hidden in attics.
Dying days hand out blindfolds
or Jack-in-the-Boxes to survivors
and to the next generation.

Drills know all about the reader
and the writer too, as eyes witness here.
Flash cards and jumping Jacks fit
within routines for a reason.

When habits help with identity,
protégés come running to jog
a place in the day to craft living room.

O Day

The loopy universe gave rise to loopy
species in a loopy solar system.

Habit, routine, practice, performance,
stage by stage—

A life in a bow blossom
highlights through emergence;
to offer a gift, one petal energizes
for the shoestrings, the ribbons, the fray.

The clock on the wall corkscrews.
Entranced months and seasons
dizzy with a few minor RX bums
and rash behaviors.

Drinking bubbly champagne
from a tumbler stains with Olympian
rings under a circus tent,
well-shaped somersaults,
tumbling a present into a not knot.

Meme Planet

To maintain ignorant city innocence
when neighbors killed neighbors,
a human sacrifice seemed to self-select
and offered distraction to the meme mob,
who sniffed for and preyed on the meek.

Compensation committees elevated
into a god, each from the long dog line,
and the bandage healed
until forgotten each epoch, each culture.

Over and over the doggods rolled.

Then a bark declared not guilty,
and business bullets flew:

"Join where and when fingers point;"

"on Earth, offer cheeks for peace."

A 3-time-denier club repents still.

Rock blushes but shoulders.

Becoming

A meme tribe bushwhacks
while one-by-one members
peel off toward authenticity.
Hoping the genuine offering
stands out on the trip
and impromptu journey,
Norm needs only twinkling
terror above the identity tent.

Angst / fear!

Paralysis tools seem to senses
in an arms factory that manufactures
a possible leg up
with homemade purpose.

A stubborn noun absorbs
against lightning strikes.
A verb lashes out
with eye movement
constructing a life sentence
that defines freedom.
Mimesis for one in practice
takes on each challenge,
where every character pokes ribs
or buckles in laughter at the period.
This subject collects
in self-recognition here.

Red Letter Day

When the day winks
after a calendar eye
has been blackened,
the blame for the cruelty
passes to the pen-holder
who wastes time in life.

Witnesses doubling
as audiences on 12 pages
smile but shrug in dismay:
Some toothy and warm
while others snowy fresh.

From zero to 85 in 31025
mornings and the bucket list
begins by age 10.
Ready, set, when to begin?
Hope pinches until ouch or yikes
between twinkles lived
and possible early demise.

What to do fleshes up
into a small mound to ponder
subtract, subtract, subtract.

Waiting for goose bumps to fly.

www.ingramcontent.com/pod-product-compliance
Lightning Source LLC
Chambersburg PA
CBHW071725040426
42446CB00011B/2226